Lucid Dreaming

A Beginner's Guide to Exploring Your Dreams

Lauren Lingard

Table of Contents

Welcome to Your Dreams 1

Chapter 1: The World of Sleep 4

Chapter 2: What Is Lucid Dreaming? 16

Chapter 3: Taking Control of Your Dreams 27

Chapter 4: Benefits of Lucid Dreaming 39

Chapter 5: Dream World Adventures & Interactions 45

Chapter 6: Advanced Lucid Dreaming Techniques 52

Let Go and Dream 58

Welcome to Your Dreams

Have you ever longed to experience something you knew was truly impossible in your real life? Perhaps journeying to an expensive travel destination you have always wanted to visit, or accomplishing something even more outlandish, like flying over the Amazon forest? No matter how wild your desires may seem in real life, nothing is out of reach in your dreams. We have all experienced just how bizarre our dreams can be, even unintentionally. We find ourselves in places we have never seen before, talking to people we have never even met. Sometimes, it has such an impact on us that we wake up the following morning disappointed that it had to end. We go back to our daily lives with limited opportunities and restrictions that prevent us from having these experiences. We wish we could recreate the dreams, but they elude us.

Now, imagine that everything you experience in a dream is under your control. You no longer have to fall asleep hoping to see or feel something with only a small chance that it will come true. Since the dream world does not adhere to the rules of real life, you can experience quite literally anything that you desire without leaving it up to chance. With the right approach, everything is within your control—your actions, the surroundings, the people, etc.

Since even regular dreams stump scientific explanations at times, it is no wonder lucid dreaming has been baffling the human species for our entire existence. Throughout the history of various cultures around the world, many references to lucid dreaming have been made. Many people used to think it was a skill special to them—a gift from the divine. Others associated the ability to control one's dreams with a spiritual out-of-body experience. With our somewhat ambiguous current understanding of this phenomenon, people's varying beliefs are not disputed.

There are countless theories, hypotheses, and studies being explored on a regular basis in search of a solid definition that would completely explain lucid dreaming. Due to the relatively uncommon nature of lucid dreaming, scientists have yet to fully explain this phenomenon, but through science, experience, and history, people are getting closer to perfecting the art of lucid dreaming. Although there is nothing completely conclusive as of yet, people continue to eagerly explore lucid dreaming on their own. As they learn the necessary skills, they often become eager to provide others with resources that would help them do the same. They recount many experiences and abilities that are similar throughout nearly everyone's lucid dreams, making it easier to construct helpful advice for those that wish to try it. With effective techniques, anyone can unlock what many people believe to be a sort of 'superpower' and extend their experiences past waking life.

It is something that at first seems so unbelievable that experiencing it feels nearly magical. After all, it is the concept of being awake in a world created by your own subconscious. We usually experience a very clear boundary between being awake and being asleep, but with lucid dreaming, this boundary gets blurred, and our two worlds are blended together. For most people, this evidently takes some getting used to. Once they do, however, the number of things they can experience becomes limitless. This is why so many people wish to learn about accessing their abilities to control their own dreams. The awareness that someone gains during a dream and the ability to control the outcome of that dream makes the experience feel extremely life-like. With modern life leaving most people busy up to the very last minute of their waking lives, who would not want a fascinating, otherworldly extension of their regular life?

Even more spectacularly, the benefits of lucid dreaming do not end when the person wakes up. Lucid dreaming has all sorts of positive effects even on the lives we lead while awake. Everyone who practices it is left with unbelievable memories and benefits to their minds. The ability to explore a tremendous number of experiences that are generally not available to people gives those who practice lucid dreaming a broader and more expansive outlook on life. Those who practice lucid dreaming tend to wake up and live life with a different perspective than those who do not.

Lucid dreaming is indisputably life changing. As humans, we get comfortable accessing only parts of our brains. To most of us, our subconscious can be a scary and confusing place—a part of our brain that is not even under our control; it stores memories we are not aware of, underlying thoughts that influence our emotions, and an imagination that we rarely end up utilizing. But as you will discover, the subconscious needn't seem so scary. With the help of lucid dreaming, you will soon be able to safely delve deep into the subconscious and explore a whole new and exciting world!

Chapter 1: The World of Sleep

Sleep is a natural part of life. It is a period of rejuvenation, healing, and rest that is critical for all living creatures. Unfortunately, in the modern world, it has become more of an accessory rather than a requirement. Within their busy lives, many people see sleep as something they only partake in when their body truly gives out; they sleep the minimal amount that will give them enough energy to continue completing their daily tasks. This is the reality for a large majority of people, with most being forced into this sort of lifestyle by the many demands of their jobs, studies, or family matters. Modern society has been making it extremely difficult for people to view sleep as the priority that it should always be. In the wild, nearly all other species of animals have built their lives centered around getting enough sleep. Luckily for them, they also are not forced to pay off bills and debt. For people, that is obviously not the case, leaving us to be the only creatures on Earth who lack sleep on such a major level. So many of us have fallen into such a wrecked sleep schedule that even when given the opportunity to get more sleep, we will choose not to.

Since sleep is one of the most critical aspects of both physical and mental health, and crucial for achieving success, it is ironic that many people who prioritize their success still end up putting sleep at the bottom of their to-do list. Quite counterproductively, such individuals may sleep for a mere six hours in favor of getting up early and hitting the gym before they head to work. But getting physical exercise, eating balanced meals, drinking enough water, and maintaining proper hygiene will never be enough if someone is sacrificing their sleep to make time for these other healthy activities. This generally happens because many people continue to look at sleep as an energy booster and nothing more; when in reality, sleep is responsible for so many healing functions that it acts as a slow but critical antidote for nearly any health problem. It may not cure every disease on its own, but without it, the problem is almost always destined to get worse. It is a fascinating tool that requires as little effort as closing our eyes and letting our minds drift away from our waking lives.

Healthy Sleep

The benefits of sleep are almost limitless, and it would require several books to list and explain them all. It is a well-known fact that an average of eight hours of sleep per night is recommended in order to live a healthy and satisfying life. This fact has become more of a hypothetical goal than one that most people actually put in effort to achieve. In the United States, as many as 35.2% of adults do not get enough sleep on a regular basis. We tend to separate these people into two categories: those whose horribly demanding lives simply leave them no time to sleep and those who consciously put off going to bed at a reasonable hour. As easy as it would be to just blame the latter group for their own choices leading to their lack of sleep, the reality is much more complex.

Work, school, and other daily tasks are not the only ones that influence a person's sleep schedule. There are a lot of barriers that make sleeping enough hours a difficult choice for many. One of those barriers is the lack of time that people find to partake in activities that they want to do outside of their work. In other words, they come home in the evening after a busy day and spend hours watching movies, doing a hobby, or socializing with others at the expense of their sleep. Although this is a conscious choice these individuals make, it is an extremely understandable one.

With only 24 hours in the day, making time and finding the desire to go to sleep earlier is not such an easy task.

Getting the right amount of sleep leads to massive physical benefits that span nearly every organ and function of our body. One of these benefits is the improvement that our immune systems undergo while we sleep. Within the human body, the immune system is a network containing the critical tools used to fight against any harmful sicknesses that we may experience. Without it, we would easily succumb to even the most common illnesses. During sleep, our body signals to the immune system to produce small proteins called cytokines which aid in strengthening and improving critical immune system cells as well as blood cells. One of these immune system cells are T cells, which are primarily responsible for circulating throughout the body and finding any potentially harmful foreign pathogens. Once the T cells identify these pathogens, they activate the body's attack against them by stimulating B cells to produce the required antibodies. Without adequate sleep, the production of T cells falls and increases the chance of not only illness but also the development of allergies.

Another benefit of sleep includes a decreased likelihood of weight gain. This occurs because the duration of sleep directly correlates to the production of hunger-regulating hormones such as ghrelin and leptin. The former stimulates our appetites and hunger while the latter lets our bodies know when we have consumed enough food to fuel us and prevents us from continuing to eat past a healthy capacity. When we do not get enough sleep, the production of ghrelin is increased (making us hungrier) while the production of leptin is decreased (making us more susceptible to overeating). In addition, people who sleep less tend to rely on caffeinated and energy-boosting foods and beverages that will help them conquer their drowsiness. This effectively puts them at risk of consuming more calories than are required for a healthy life, possibly leading to weight-related health issues in the future.

With less than an adequate amount of sleep, our hearts are also put at risk. This occurs due to the overproduction of the stress hormone cortisol resulting from short sleep durations. Cortisol then causes the heart to work harder than necessary, which can bring about high blood pressure, heart disease, type 2 diabetes, and even heart attacks.

Just like the health of our hearts and immune systems relies on adequate sleep, so do our brains. A person's psychological state is deeply affected by the amount of time they spend sleeping. Less sleep is directly tied to increased chances of depression, anxiety, and even bipolar disorder. On a less extreme side, lack of sleep also causes an increase in stress levels and feelings of anxiousness or nervousness throughout the day. The lack of energy can often make the individual react more severely to hardships in their life than they would if they had gotten enough sleep. Sleep deprivation can also lead to a lack of attention, worsened memory, and not surprisingly, a decrease in productivity.

There is a small and intriguing part of the population that is able to function completely fine on less than six hours of sleep. Unfortunately, this only applies to as little as an estimated 5% of the population. This has been linked to a mutation of the gene DEC2 that allows their bodies to get all the benefits of sleep in a considerably shorter amount of time than the general population. This rare genetic mutation lets people fall asleep as late as midnight, wake up as early as four in the morning, and feel more refreshed than an average person would after six hours of sleep. On the other side of the sleep spectrum are, more commonly, people who suffer from various sleep disorders, an extremely challenging struggle that can lead to any of the health problems described above. The wide variety of identified sleep disorders including insomnia, sleep apnea, and others affects between 50 and 70 million adults in the United States. Without the right medical care and treatment, these disorders can have many risky health complications.

For others that are unable to sufficiently manage their sleep schedules, it is not a biological disorder that is to blame but generally a rigid force of habit. This includes aspects such as their dependence on technological devices and social media, as well as feelings of stress or restlessness in the evening. People that struggle with such elements should consider the following steps towards improving their sleep:

- Limit your screen time before bed by setting boundaries. Provide a window of time for yourself to enjoy the media of your choice, guilt-free. When the time is up, put away the distracting devices and allow yourself to focus on getting physically and mentally ready to fall asleep. In fact, blue light emitted by such devices shifts people's circadian rhythms and decreases the body's production of melatonin, making it harder for a person to fall asleep.

- Establish and stick to a solid sleep routine. Many people claim they do not get enough sleep simply because they do not feel tired until a much later hour. Avoid scheduling physically demanding activities close to your ideal bedtime, as they lessen the feeling of tiredness for hours to come. Also, try to go to bed around the same time every night. By being consistent with the appropriate sleep schedule seven days of the week, your body will get used to this routine and start naturally nudging you towards going to bed at a reasonable hour.

- Give yourself time to wind down and de-stress before bed. Keep a journal, have a calming cup of tea, or meditate to provide yourself a space to release all the anxieties floating around in your mind. By letting your feelings out, you are less likely to be bombarded by them while you are trying to fall asleep.

The Cycle of Sleep

While we sleep, we undergo cycle after cycle of various stages of sleep. Each one is unique from the others and provides us with its own experiences and sleep benefits. On average, a person will go through four to six full sleep cycles in one night. These cycles happen continuously and are influenced by our biological pattern of brain waves. In fact, many people rely on counting sleep cycles rather than hours in order to verify that they are getting enough sleep. The first cycle experienced during a night of sleep is generally the shortest of the bunch, generally lasting anywhere between 70 and 100 minutes, while the later cycles range from 90 to 120 minutes in length. The length and quality of each stage of the cycle is influenced by a person's age, previous quality of sleep, and even consumption of alcohol. There are four total stages in the sleep cycle, beginning with three various stages of non-rapid eye movement sleep—also known as quiescent sleep—and ending with rapid eye movement sleep.

Each stage is important for understanding the basics of lucid dreaming. When you are aware of what occurs during each stage, you will learn at what times during the night you are most likely to dream. Furthermore, it will unveil the times at which lucidity within a dream is most possible and tell you when you will be able to become conscious in your dream.

Stage 1: NREM1

The first stage within the sleep cycle is non-rapid eye movement stage one, abbreviated as NREM1. This stage occurs in the very beginning of sleep, right as you begin to doze off. Before NREM1 and while we are awake and alert, our brain produces gamma and beta waves. These two waves generally signal our engagement and complex thought processes. During NREM1, however, the brain emits alpha and theta waves. Alpha waves can also be emitted while a person is awake, usually after they take a mental break using meditation or another calming activity. In the first half of the NREM1 cycle, low-frequency alpha waves slightly dominate in the frontal lobe of the brain. This indicates a strong sense of relaxation while the person is still relatively awake, and their brain is still active. As the person slips further into sleep during the second half of NREM1, more theta waves with larger amplitudes and even lower frequencies start being produced by the brain. During this stage, a person's heart rate and breathing slow down while their core body temperature slightly drops. Their muscles become increasingly more relaxed and may even slightly twitch. NREM1 generally lasts a very short time, ranging from five to ten minutes. People woken up during this stage of sleep often report not having been asleep yet.

Stage 2: NREM2

The second stage of non-rapid eye movement sleep is NREM2. This stage is longer than NREM1, lasting anywhere between 30 and 60 minutes. During NREM2, the person's body and mind go into a much deeper state of relaxation. They fall away further from waking reality and become less aware of their surroundings. Their eye movements stop, their body temperature continues to slightly fall, and breathing and heart rate return to their regular rhythms. The brain continues emitting the theta waves it began emitting in the second half of NREM1, except with short bursts of brain activity called spindles. Such sleep spindles are powerful yet brief moments of high frequency brain waves, lasting less than two seconds. These quick spindles during NREM1 are very important for a person's learning and memory abilities. In particular, they occur when your brain is going over and consolidating anything that you may have learned or practiced while you were awake the previous day. Parallel to sleep spindles are K-complexes—delta frequency brain waves with a significantly large amplitude. Similar to spindles, they are not constant throughout all of NREM2 and only occur when a person experiences any external stimuli while sleeping.

Stage 3: NREM3

After the preparation and gradual relaxation that the body and mind go through during NREM1 and NREM2, comes the final stage of non-rapid eye movement sleep, NREM3. This stage is the beginning of deep sleep, otherwise known as slow-wave sleep (SWS). This is because during the duration of NREM3, the brain's activity slows down even further by producing delta waves. Delta waves are the slowest waves a human brain is capable of producing. They can sometimes be stimulated through binaural beats prior to bed to help the individual's brain produce them during NREM3 and REM. This beginning of deep sleep causes external stimuli to no longer affect the sleeping individual, making it considerably harder to wake them up. Breathing and heart rates both slow down dramatically during this stage once again, pushing the individual into a very strong physical relaxation. It is during this stage that the body begins to repair any physical issues and improve health. Furthermore, the brain continues to solidify any information it has received over the course of the last day, similar to what spindles do during NREM2.

Stage 4: REM

The last stage of sleep is arguably the most well-known, called rapid eye movement or REM sleep. It also falls into the category of slow-wave sleep, as does NREM3. It is during this stage that dreams are most commonly and vividly experienced. REM sleep generally begins 90 minutes after a person falls asleep and its duration increases in length with each repeating cycle. In the first cycle, REM sleep lasts around a mere 10 minutes, but goes all the way up to 60 minutes in the last cycle. However, the older a person gets, the shorter their average REM stage becomes. During this stage, the body focuses on tasks such as building and strengthening bones, improving the immune system, and repairing tissue. In addition to the brain continuing its information turnover just like in NREM3, the REM stage is also important for the brain to process emotional information as well. This often influences the emotional environment of the dreams experienced by the individual.

Interestingly, brain activity during the REM stage of sleep is very similar to its activity during the hours the person spends awake. This indicates that the brain is actively engaged during REM sleep by producing dreams. The brain waves being produced at this stage are still largely delta waves; individuals who experience more alpha waves during NREM3 and REM sleep tend to feel less refreshed after waking up. Unlike the brain, however, physical muscles of the individual are completely immobilized during the REM stage of sleep. This effectively prevents the individual from physically acting on what they experience in their dreams. The combination of high brain activity and physical paralysis have come to make REM sleep also be known as paradoxical sleep. While the first three stages of the sleep cycle are mostly aimed at relaxation and minor restorative processes, lucid dreaming is best experienced during REM sleep.

Sleep Paralysis

An undesirable and often intimidating experience during sleep is that of sleep paralysis. Sleep paralysis is when a person is conscious but unable to move their muscles. They often see their surrounding environment, are able to think complex thoughts and accurately process emotions, but simultaneously feel physically paralyzed. This can occur both while a person is trying to fall asleep or just as they are waking up; however, the latter occurs more commonly. It has been estimated that only 8% of the population will ever go through an episode of sleep paralysis. There is not enough data that provides information on how often these people will have recurring sleep paralysis, however some believe that it occurs more often in people that have sleeping disorders such as insomnia.

In the past, sleep paralysis was, not surprisingly, attributed to paranormal activity. People believed it was ghosts, demons, or other ill-willing entities that would paralyze the individual and proceed to scare them. Although the truth behind sleep paralysis still confuses most, neurologists and psychologists have found many scientific explanations that can put people who experience it at ease. For the most part, it is believed that sleep paralysis is simply a biological delay between your body waking up and your mind. As unsettling as sleep paralysis may be, its causes are nothing paranormal. Instead, it is a natural reaction of your brain that occurs between a state of being fully asleep and fully awake.

If a person experiences sleep paralysis while falling asleep, it is called hypnagogic sleep paralysis. This occurs when the body and mind are actively falling asleep until the person's brain is brought back to its waking state and the person becomes suddenly aware. This leaves them mentally alert while their body continues its transition into sleep. Sleep paralysis that happens when a person is waking up after a sleep cycle is called hypnopompic sleep paralysis. The concept here is similar, but instead of taking place during the first few stages of sleep it happens when a person becomes prematurely alert prior to the full completion of the REM stage. As previously explored, muscles during the REM stage of sleep become immobilized. Therefore, if a person's brain returns to a conscious state of mind during this stage, they cannot voluntarily move or speak.

What often makes this experience eerie is the presence of hallucinations, both hypnagogic and hypnopompic. Both hypnagogic and hypnopompic hallucinations take place on their own but also during their respective forms of sleep paralysis. Together, hypnagogic and hypnopompic hallucinations are referred to as hypnagogia. The neurological signs of hypnagogia are similar to both daydreams and nighttime dreams. When this happens at the same time as sleep paralysis, it leaves the person experiencing immobility while also seeing, hearing, or even feeling sensations that are not real, very similar to that of a dream. This can be a very distressing experience, especially considering the individual has no control over their physical movements. Unfortunately, due to their conscious awareness, these hallucinations are often vivid and feel extremely real. When hypnagogia occurs frequently, it may be a sign of a sleep disorder called parasomnia and may require help from a professional.

The connection of hypnagogia, sleep paralysis, and lucid dreaming is quite interesting. Although the common definition of lucid dreaming describes it as something that happens when a person is deep in the REM stage of sleep, similar experiences have been recorded during episodes of sleep paralysis. The person can have what is described as out of body experiences and even feel detached from their physical form. During sleep paralysis, this sensation of lucid dreaming is evidently accompanied by various hypnagogia. Overall, sleep paralysis is more likely to occur when the person was previously sleep deprived.

Chapter 2: What Is Lucid Dreaming?

Understanding the world of sleep gives you the opportunity to dive into the even more complex world of lucid dreaming. Dreams in general have been a point of interest for the entirety of recorded human history. The exploration of dreams has played a part in the culture, art, and media of every civilization to date. It remains fascinating for humans—who are so used to living solely in their waking life—to have access to such a multitude of worlds nearly every night. Its persistence in human experience has made it a studied topic by many. The study of dreams is called oneirology and describes various specialists and professionals who spend their business hours focused on solving this millennia-long mystery. Psychologists, neurologists, and other scientific researchers have made much progress over the course of several centuries; however, the first time a truly neurological approach was used took place only in the mid-20th century when researchers Eugene Aserinsky and Nathaniel Kleitman first made the discovery of REM sleep. Since this turning point, science has been making relatively steady progress.

Even with a lack of a solid explanation, all types of dreams provide their own benefits. Unlike lucid dreaming, regular dreams come so naturally to the majority of the population that they do not even require any sort of control. People simply lie down and let their body and mind completely take over what they experience for the next several hours. There is certainly a reason for all dreams to occur; our minds show us pictures, throw us into new situations, and make us experience things we otherwise never would. Each person individually decides how much significance to assign their dreams. While many still treat them as something that just happens, others have recognized the value that exploring their dreams—lucid or otherwise—can actually bring. In order to transform your life with lucid dreaming, it is critical to examine the dreams you already have. Oftentimes, the dreams our brain creates with complete freedom can be indicators of something much bigger.

What Are Dreams?

When we sleep, our brain conjures up visual imagery, sensations, thoughts, and emotions that we experience under full subconsciousness. For creatures that are very understanding of our conscious world and quite lost in our subconsciousness, it can be quite unbelievable to know that we are able to see and feel sensations that are not caused by tangible, external factors. Our eyes are closed, yet we see vividly; we are laying calmly in our beds, yet we feel our body moving as we run in our dreams. This is the first indicator of just how much our brains are capable of all by themselves. What causes further confusion is why and how these experiences vary so wildly even from one night to the next. At times, they are so pleasant that we wish our waking lives to be more like them, while at others we cannot wait to wake up.

Dreams most often occur during REM sleep, although it is possible for them to appear in non-REM stages of sleep as well. While we dream, especially during REM, our brain's emotional sectors are considerably more activated than those in charge of logical thinking. Specifically, our prefrontal cortex is much less active while we sleep. This is often used to explain why so many of our dreams are completely irrational and would make no sense in real life—the scenarios and our reactions to them are much more emotionally driven. Dreams that occur in non-REM stages are generally more coherent and may have more connections to real life. Some common attributes of REM dreams include:

- experiencing everything in the first-person perspective

- scenarios are produced without any conscious effort

- content is often surreal and unlike real life

- interactions with other people whether they are identifiable or not

- certain elements can be similar to that of the dreamer's real life

A study that focused on learning about characters within people's dreams found that 49% of the people that appeared in dreams were someone that the dreamer knew relatively well, 35% were only identifiable by their role in the dream, and 16% were completely unidentifiable. Interestingly, even those 51% of characters that did not have an identifiable connection to the dreamer have been seen by them in real life. In other words, every face that we see in our dreams is one that our eyes have caught at one point or another, whether we remember consciously or not. This fact further proves that our brains are using various stored subconscious knowledge to influence the created dream. While there are a lot of commonalities among general dreams, many people have very individual experiences. For example, some people only dream in black and white while others see a full spectrum of colors.

Just like REM stages in the first few cycles of sleep, dreams tend to be shorter at first and then get longer with each cycle. Dreams tend to last anywhere between 5 to 20 minutes each, with the average person experiencing between 3 and 6 dreams per night. However, due to the specialized functioning of our brains during REM sleep, our information rarely gets processed and stored correctly, causing us to forget nearly 95% of our dreams as soon as we wake up.

Why Do We Dream?

There remains no outright explanation as to why we may experience dreams. Both average people and professionals offer a multitude of reasons, with each one being a candidate for a solid explanation. Although many experts do not agree, most base their conclusions on past psychologists' works as well as modern scientific revelations. Some common theories on why we dream include:

- our brain uses dreams to consolidate memories

- emotions are practiced and processed based on the new scenarios the dream creates

- our brain clears out any unnecessary information

- dreams may contain replayed situations from real life for the brain to analyze

- dreams are just a byproduct of sleeping and have no inherent use

Regardless of which theory may be later deemed correct, the fact remains that most dreams are quite autobiographical and are strongly influenced by the dreamer's life. This includes people they know, conversations they have had, and recent life circumstances.

A lot of theories—especially those from psychologists' point of view—center around dreams as serving the role of a mini therapy session. They give the person the opportunity to confront a strong emotion that they have been experiencing while awake, sometimes even allowing them to realize certain emotional connections that would otherwise be absent. This is because during REM sleep, our brain has very low levels of noradrenaline—a hormone that stimulates our feelings of anxiety. This can further aid the brain in processing difficult emotions without as much fear as it would incur while awake. For dreams that cause the person a lot of fear or even panic, the person may be faced with a different psychological task of practicing their reaction to danger. In particular, such uneasy dreams may be used by the brain to practice its fight or flight response. This theory is further supported by the fact that the amygdala is one of the most active parts of the brain during REM sleep. Being known for its service of indicating fear, the amygdala's considerable activity therefore indicates that the brain is testing our preparedness for a potential threat.

Other people believe that creative boosts are our dream's central purpose. This is often tied to our brain's extremely emotional rather than logical thinking for the duration of REM sleep. In comparison to the barriers that our logic may impose on us while awake, our sleeping brains allow us to think creatively with less limits. In fact, Dmitri Mendeleev—the creator of the periodic table—stated that the idea for his creation came to him as a visual image in a dream.

Other than the purposes of dreams, a long-debated topic has been why dreams take certain forms and not others. Reportedly, 43% of American adults believe that our dreams showcase our subconscious desires and emotions. While there are many dreams that are completely unique to the individual experiencing them, there are also ones that seem to happen across a large majority of the population. The following is a list of such dreams and potential explanations as to what they may symbolize:

- Dreams about falling are widely reported and are believed to indicate that there is an area of real life in which you have been particularly struggling

- Dreams about appearing naked in public spaces is often associated with feeling out of place in your community or being uncomfortable with your flaws

- Dreams that contain a motif of being chased are often thought to indicate that there is an uncomfortable or fear-inducing problem that you are avoiding in real life

- Dreams in which you lose teeth are particularly common and are associated with being insecure in your physical appearance or communication skills

- Dreams that include flying can represent either the feeling of freedom, or on the flip side, the desire to escape something in real life

Carl Jung & Sigmund Freud

The names of Carl Jung and Sigmund Freud are heavily associated with psychology. What a lot of people do not assign as much notice to, however, is their powerful theories on why humans dream and whether or not doing so is crucial to their development and well-being. Although Jung and Freud were known to be good friends and colleagues, their debate on the conceptualization of dreams may have actually pushed them to eventually end their friendship.

Sigmund Freud notoriously believed that people's dreams represent their darkest, innermost desires—mainly sexual repression. He argued that while we sleep, the tactics we generally use to remain reserved stop working and allow the brain to explore everything that it desires, no matter how taboo.

Carl Jung, on the other hand, did not believe in Freud's idea that dreams almost always represent our cravings in relation to sexuality, although he did support the theory that our dreams were symbolic of our unconscious mind. Jung also agreed with Freud that dreams could be used by our brains to re-assess certain past events, but his theory also stated that they could give us information on what to expect from ourselves in the future. A lot of modern theories are based on a combination of elements from both Freud's and Jung's perspectives on dreams.

Types of Dreams

Professionals have currently established five main categories of dreams. What they all have in common is the person entering a different state of mind and allowing their subconscious to take over their thoughts and visualizations. With this in mind, it comes as no surprise that dreams do not only occur at night.

Normal dreams are those that most often occur during REM sleep and have already been described. The second, often overlooked category of dreams, however, is daydreams. A lot of people do not even realize that daydreams—a very common phenomenon—are officially recognized as a type of dream. Although this number tends to decrease with age, throughout the day, the average person can spend over 30% of their time daydreaming. The truth is this statistic may seem a little exaggerated to most people solely because we often do not even recognize when we daydream. Daydreaming often occurs as we accidentally let our mind wander from our tasks or surroundings to a world of thought that lightly blocks out external stimuli. Daydreams are further categorized into two types: positive-constructive and dysphoric. Positive-constructive dreams, as the name implies, generally includes positive visualizations and sensations. People who tend to engage in this type of daydreaming are believed to be more prone to creativity and can even have an easier time lucid dreaming. Dysphoric daydreaming, however, involves imagining undesirable outcomes and can lead to anxiety.

The next type of dream is false awakenings. During these dreams, a person may feel as if they have woken up. In other words, they feel as if they are awake and proceed to start their morning in a regular way, until they either realize it is still a dream or they wake up for real. In false awakenings, the surroundings created by the dream are incredibly life-like, making the person feel as if they have truly woken up. Interestingly, some people who have false awakenings report experiencing multiple ones in a row.

Nightmares are the fourth type of dreams and are generally normal dreams that end up providing a terrifying experience. The reason they are so effective in their horror is because the person is not aware that they are dreaming and that everything that seems so scary is not actually real. Furthermore, some nightmares are so intense that the person can even experience hallucinations of feeling pain without any external cause. The cause for nightmares is not clear; however, distress, illness, and consumption of alcohol or drugs may increase their likelihood. Although nightmares affect children more, between 2% and 8% of adults struggle with chronic nightmares. The cause of chronic nightmares has yet to be pinpointed, but side effects of some medications could be to blame. In other cases, people can have more nightmares if they have eaten close to bedtime. This could be due to the metabolism sending certain signals to the brain that increase its activity. For those who suffer from chronic nightmares, some people actually recommend learning lucid dreaming techniques to help alleviate the feelings of helplessness and terror experienced during nightmares.

Lucid Dreams

Lucid dreams are the fifth and final category of dreams. They are defined as regular dreams that occur while asleep, in which the individual is aware that they are dreaming and can potentially even control the dream entirely. For obvious reasons, those that are naturally inclined towards lucid dreaming are the envy of those that want to learn. The good news is, although lucid dreams are significantly rarer than other types of dreams, they are not out of your reach. In fact, as many as 55% of people are said to have experienced a lucid dream at one point or another.

A lot of people who are unaware of, or are new to, this phenomenon harbor a lot of fear in relation to it. They are scared of panicking and getting stuck in the dream, not knowing what to do, or even dying in real life. This is not surprising, considering people always tend to fear what they do not know. Luckily, with the control they have over their dreams, a lucid dreamer is able to avoid both panicking and getting stuck, and dying in real life is simply impossible. People who have experienced lucid dreaming often feel a sense of peace and serenity when they become aware that they are dreaming, not panic.

However, it is worth noting that lucid dreaming should not only be treated as an amusement park. Most people who lucid dream are extremely in tune with their inner selves and subconsciousness even prior to attempting it. For this reason, it is recommended that people use lucid dreaming for purposes other than solely fulfilling their wildest dreams. Instead, they are encouraged to focus on expanding their perspectives and ideas and engaging a generally more inaccessible part of their brain.

Lucid dreaming tackles the boundary between our real world and our dreams. Furthermore, it explores the relationship between the subconscious and conscious parts of our minds. Scientifically speaking, parts of our brain—such as the prefrontal cortex—become more activated during lucid dreams than regular dreams. This allows our brains to become logical during lucid dreams—something that does not happen during regular dreaming.

The hardest aspect of lucid dreaming tends to be controlling it. In fact, even avid lucid dreamers are still sometimes unable to control every aspect of the dream; they may successfully control their own actions or characters while their subconscious still dictates other aspects. Generally, the more you become comfortable with lucid dreaming, the easier this practice gets.

History & Perspectives

The term lucid dreaming was coined in 1913, by Dutch psychiatrist Frederik van Eeden. A lot of the scientific research that came with the phenomenon occurred later, between the 1960s and the 1980s. However, the roots of lucid dreaming do not only lie in science. Though lucid dreaming is directly tied to the biological functioning of the human brain, many people use it to their own advantage for spiritual or even solely entertainment purposes. In fact, there is massive overlap between spirituality and lucid dreaming. In Buddhism, for example, some people practice lucid dreaming with the goal of increasing their connection to spirituality. This practice includes learning to become aware while dreaming and completing certain tasks important to inner growth; some people choose to use lucid dreaming to face certain fears while others may even attempt to interact with a spiritual figure. Lucid dreaming has been used for similar purposes for thousands of years and spans multiple spiritualities and cultures. A lot of people who use lucid dreaming in these ways have combined it with meditation in the waking world.

Chapter 3: Taking Control of Your Dreams

Many people who are not professionals in the field of neuroscience, psychology, or dream research tend to desire experiencing lucid dreams solely for their own personal advantage; they may be using it for spiritual reasons, improving cognitive functions, overcoming trauma, or just expanding their experiences. In fact, from researchers' point of view, more lucid dreaming could also lead to a better understanding of our conscious and subconscious minds. Lucid dreaming is actually a relatively common method of therapy for people who suffer from post-traumatic stress disorder (PTSD). Since distressing events could potentially cause chronic nightmares, being able to control these dreadful experiences through lucid dreaming can be the key to eventually stopping them from occurring altogether.

A point of concern regarding lucid dreaming is that people who engage in it too often may become confused between reality and their dreams. For this reason, it is recommended to use lucid dreaming not as a means to escape the difficulties of the real world, but to improve your perspective. For people who are keen on learning the tricks of lucid dreaming without a professional or therapist, building a solid foundation is the first step. This entails a period of self-reflection and a willingness to explore your subconscious mind without underlying fears or doubts. A person who is completely disconnected from their subconscious risks having more difficulty or even unpleasant lucid dreaming experiences. In other words, being in the right state of mind prior to incorporating lucid dreaming techniques is key. There are studies that have found that a person's willingness to experience lucid dreaming has a direct correlation on the phenomenon, even increasing its frequency of occurrence.

People with spiritual inclination also have a generally easier time achieving lucid dreams due to their experience with their subconscious. For example, the Buddhist monks who use lucid dreaming as a means of strengthening their connection to spirituality often practice meditation throughout the day. This daytime activity prompts the brain to create alpha waves outside of just the beginning stages of NREM sleep. When combining both meditation and lucid dreaming throughout their 24 hours, they are also improving their brain's network between various states of consciousness and relaxation.

Getting Started

A person who holds no memory or emotional ties to their dreams is at the very beginning of their journey. If you are someone who is at square one, it is important to learn about your current dreams prior to trying to achieve lucidity. Without the ability to recollect your regular dreams, lucid dreaming techniques will have almost no use as you are very out of touch with the world of your dreams. In order to change this, begin by learning about the dreams your mind produces on its own before taking matters into your own hands.

Dream Recall

We have all experienced this—you wake up from a dream convinced that it was so impactful and memorable that there is no way you would forget it in the morning; you then get up and start your day and quickly come across the nagging feeling that you dreamt something remarkable with absolutely no recollection of it. It can be quite an unsettling feeling to know that the memory of your dream that was once so vivid slipped away in mere minutes or even seconds. Although part of this is evidently your brain chemistry's fault, there are ways to improve your dream recall—something that is critical for future lucid dreaming.

As already mentioned, REM stages become longer as the night progresses, with the interval between each REM stage becoming shorter. Using this information, you have the ability to predict the times at which you will be experiencing REM sleep throughout your night. If you wake from REM sleep, there is a 95% probability that you were dreaming and will be able to describe it in detail. If you are able to wake yourself during your REM periods, you will have a much easier time tapping into the memory you have of your dreams. For example, if you set an alarm for sometime during the last two hours of your sleep, there is a good chance you will wake up with a highly accurate dream recall. At first, waking up mid-dream may seem counterintuitive. After all, lucid dreaming occurs while still asleep and can be exceptionally enjoyable, so how can such an interruption improve lucidity? The answer is quite simple—waking up and then going back to sleep to the same dream is significantly easier in the REM stage of sleep than any other.

To further increase your chances for dream recall, make sure to set an intention prior to falling asleep. This may sound too simple to work; however, even something as easy as thinking about remembering your future dream can truly make your brain work harder to remember it. All it takes is telling yourself something along the lines of 'I will remember my dream' as you get into bed and close your eyes. Although it might take a few tries, this method has been used by many people to wake up with a fresh and lasting memory of their dreams.

Our physical body has recollection abilities as well, and dream memories can even be stored in our muscles. If you are able to stay in the same position that you wake up in until you remember your dream, you will have far better recall results. If you are forced to shift your body, to switch off your alarm for instance, then immediately return to the position your body was in before. Sometimes, we wake up with only a small portion or singular detail in our recollection of a dream. Perhaps it is a person you remember seeing or a location. When this happens, you can attempt to work backwards from what it is you remember by asking yourself insightful questions the moment you wake up. You can use that tiny piece of a memory to unlock others, since dream threads are all connected. If you remember yourself trying on a piece of clothing, for example, analyze it further: What color was it? Where were you trying it on? Did you like or dislike it? These nitty gritty details may echo further fragmented dream memories. Other times, it is not even a dream vision that you may remember at all; sometimes, it is a feeling that your dream caused you to wake up with. By tuning into that feeling of happiness, turmoil, anger, or whatever it may be, you may get dream recall flashes that will provide the bigger picture.

The last, and most popular, technique for dream recall is a dream journal. The explanation is right there in the name—it is a sort of diary in which you write down as much as you can remember from your dreams. The key here is consistency; reach for that dream journal at any point of time in which you wake up, be it in the middle of the night or in the morning. Focus on the emotions and themes of the dream, not just the visual events that unfolded. Over the course of some time, you will likely begin to see meaningful connections between emotions and events in your dream, indicating some recurring symbolism. Through consistent dream journaling, you not only train your brain to dig for those memories, but you also make the territory of your dreams feel considerably more familiar.

Reality Testing

In order to improve your chances at lucid dreaming, it is important to be skilled at differentiating between reality and your dreams. As simple as that may sound at first, our dreams may sometimes feel so realistic that you would not even assume you are dreaming. However, there are specific elements that you could look out for that will give away whether you are dreaming or awake. The process of this differentiation is called reality testing.

Our brains are imperfect and often do not have a fully accurate recollection of real life. Therefore, as realistic as they may cause our dreams to be, they often fail at reproducing some small details. By knowing what these details may be and verifying them, you will make it easier for yourself to identify when you are dreaming. Some examples of effective reality tests include:

- Checking your hands. Begin by lifting up your hand and examining it; proceed to look elsewhere and bring your eyes back to it again. If the features of your hand have not changed in any way, you are not dreaming. Within dreams, the brain is not capable of producing the same visual image of your hand twice in a row; oftentimes it could have extra fingers or become blurred.

- Trying to touch or handle something in a way that would be impossible in real life. For example, attempt to reach through your arm—something that is obviously impossible in real life. If your hand reaches through it with ease, you know you are dreaming.

- Attempting to coherently read a piece of text. It is extremely rare for you to be able to read and speak out loud in a dream, due to your brain's optic nerve not being able to function as it does while you are awake.

- Trying to use a digital device normally. In a dream, technology does not function anywhere near how it does in real life. This is because our brain is familiar with such devices, but evidently does not correctly comprehend how they work. This could manifest itself as a phone screen turning liquid, or the app icons physically jumping across the page, for example.

- Checking the time on a clock. For some reason, clocks are a very difficult thing for the brain to accurately replicate. Some theorize that this is because the brain does not naturally process time the way we force it to while awake. With this in mind, clocks in a dream will either look unnaturally shaped, show a wildly different time every time you look at it, or count time in a bizarre fashion.

- Turning the lights in a room on or off. Sometimes, the light switch will not work properly. It may function erratically and unlike it would in real life.

The idea of completing reality checks has to do with how our brain renders dreams. Our brains constantly put in effort to maintain the dream world that they have created but struggle to replicate the small details that we are used to in real life. When dreaming, attempting to perfectly replicate something in your mind or examine it will prove that it has faults. In fact, noticing these small details and flaws of imperfect rendering may help you gain awareness that you are in a dream. Reality testing is not just something that should be done solely when you assume you are in a dream. In fact, getting into the habit of doing reality tests while you are awake will increase the chances of you remembering to do them while asleep.

The subconscious part of our mind is capable of fascinating creativity and will manage to produce a wide range of aspects to include in its dream. The reason that it does not manage the small details so perfectly is because the left part of our brain is generally inactive while we are asleep—the part of our brains that we depend on to analyze detail and use logic. Looking out for dream signs that involve such precision will make it easier to distinguish between reality and the dream world. An interesting caveat is that as soon as we become lucid in our dreams, our left brain kicks back into gear within 30 seconds, turning on more of our logical thinking. This causes our brains to improve their recollection of the small details that were previously flawed. In other words, as a lucid dream progresses, reality checks become less and less reliable.

Signs In a Dream

A sign in a dream can be any sort of weird or unlikely event that can also indicate that you are in a dream. In the movie *Inception*, for example, the lead character Dom spins a top to discern whether he is in a dream or if he is in the waking world. If it spins normally and topples over as usual, he knows that he is awake;

however, if the top keeps on spinning and spinning for an endless amount of time, he recognizes that he is not awake. Sometimes, signs that you are dreaming will be very clearly distinguished, like being able to fly, or can be more subtle, such as being a child in your dream but being aware that in real life you are much older.

The three categories of dream signs are:

1. **Anomalies**: random, one-off strange events (i.e a barking elephant)

2. **Dream themes**: very common themes and occurrences that happen in many people's dreams (i.e. being naked in public)

3. **Recurring signs**: can be unique to you and are signs that occur more than once

Becoming aware of what dream signs may be unique to you is a great way to familiarize yourself with the real world versus your dream world. If you are able to consciously notice these signs while dreaming, you will be more likely to trigger lucidity. If you are keeping a dream diary, it will be even easier for you to start noticing themes and signs unique to you that may indicate when you are dreaming. By knowing them well, you will be able to specifically look out for them in your dreams and heighten your awareness.

Popular Techniques

Whether their intention was research or therapy, professionals have created a number of various lucid dreaming techniques over the years. With this variety of techniques, almost anyone is able to test, try, and determine which one is the most effective for them. These techniques are in the very early stages of research and their efficacy therefore depends almost completely on the individual.

Mnemonic Induction of Lucid Dreams (MILD)

Anyone who has done real research on lucid dreaming and its techniques will surely come across the name Stephen LaBerge—a psychophysiologist who specializes in the study of lucid dreams. In search of an explanation for lucid dreaming, he managed to create the extremely popular technique called mnemonic induction of lucid dreams (MILD), centered around the use of memory to become lucid. This technique is widely used as one of the best for becoming lucid within a dream. It often uses elements of visualization, self-hypnosis, and one's capability of remembering to do a certain action in the future, a phenomenon called prospective memory. Although he has popularized the MILD method in modern times, LaBerge actually created it through inspiration using old lucid dreaming techniques from the 16h century.

The MILD technique combines dream recall and prospective memory. It urges you to envision yourself being back in the dream even though you are currently awake. To do this, try and recall the dream as vividly as possible and choose a particular scene that has a dream sign. In other words, if you saw a deformed clock in your dream, strongly summon it in your mind prior to going back to sleep. Once you manage to completely immerse yourself in this memory, you then proceed to set and focus on the intention to recognize that you are dreaming. Following these actions, the probability of you becoming lucid in your next REM stage is very high.

Prospective memory, a key part of the MILD technique, is actually a part of our day-to-day life, like when we remind ourselves of something we must complete in the near future. You may have already experienced a similar power before; you tell yourself before sleeping that you must wake up at 7am, and the following morning you have woken up prior to the ringing of your alarm clock. Our prospective memory manages to keep our brains activated, but not consciously, allowing it to still have access to the intention we set. For lucid dreaming, prospective memory increases the possibility of you becoming aware.

Wake-Initiated Lucid Dream (WILD)

The wake-initiated lucid dream (WILD) technique is supposedly one of the harder ones that Stephen LaBerge created. It is centered on the idea of remaining conscious while letting the rest of your mind and body drift into sleep. This technique includes waking yourself up after four to six hours of sleep and spending some time awake before returning to bed. Once you do, you go to bed and remain completely still, imagining that your body is melting into the surface on which you lie. Within a bit of time, hypnagogic hallucinations may begin, signaling that you are transitioning into a half-dream state. When this begins, observe the hallucinations and allow yourself to stay relaxed, further drifting off.

However, the hypnagogic hallucinations may eventually come with sleep paralysis—indicating that your body is continuing on its journey towards sleep. When this occurs, remain relaxed and remember that this is just another step towards entering a wake-induced lucid dream. After sleep paralysis, the technique generally prompts a sort of out-of-body experience by creating a dream scene that takes place in the very room that you are asleep in. For obvious reasons, people who have bad experiences with sleep paralysis or are not in a good state of mind will not favor the WILD technique due to its potential to cause unnerving sleep paralysis experiences. With this in mind, it is recommended to only attempt the WILD technique after you have mastered the easier ones.

Senses Initiated Lucid Dream (SSILD)

The senses initiated lucid dream (SSILD) technique is somewhat similar to the MILD, in that it involves waking up after around five hours of sleep before allowing yourself to go back to bed. What is different in the SSILD, however, is not focusing on the memories of a recent dream, but rather external stimuli around you. Furthermore, the SSILD technique only requires 30 to 90 seconds of being awake before going back to bed. It is recommended that while you are awake for that short time, focus intensely on the things around you that you see, hear, and feel. When you go back to sleep after directing all your focus and energy to such stimuli, your brain may carry that into the dream you return to and allow you to become lucid.

Dream Initiated Lucid Dream (DILD)

Unlike every other technique discussed thus far, the dream initiated lucid dream (DILD) does not start when you are awake; rather, it is used when the person is already dreaming, without having to wake up at all. The most popular DILD method for becoming aware in a dream is object recognition. Evidently, this technique combines the idea of reality testing and bringing awareness to the dream. All it takes is using one of the practices of reality testing and identifying any weirdness of objects to be a sign of a dream. Once you are dreaming, employ any combination of techniques for reality testing until you are convinced that they point to you being in a dream. For example, look for flawed details that may appear in your hands, clocks, or written text. As soon as you have used these details to identify that you are not awake, you become completely lucid.

Chapter 4: Benefits of Lucid Dreaming

Lucid dreaming isn't only about having wild adventures while you sleep. It also has many benefits that can spill over into your waking life. This dreaming technique can have massive positive effects on your mental, emotional, and even physical health.

The control that a person is able to accumulate through lucid dreaming often translates into waking life. In fact, people who have lucid dreams are likely to have less anxiety in their real lives. They no longer think everything around them is out of their control. They are used to taking matters into their own hands. In addition, the way that particular parts of the brain interact with each other during a lucid dream is unlike their interaction during any other state of being. With these new and strengthened connections, the brain's capability to function is often improved in the waking state as well.

Insight & Creativity

Apart from the creativity involved in taking control of a dream and potentially manipulating the outcome, there are ways that the dreaming mind can help you think outside of the box even in your daily life. Although there are no conclusive tests that show whether or not lucid dreaming increases someone's intelligence, there is evidence of other mental benefits. Most notorious of these benefits are heightened creativity and insightfulness. As previously discussed, lucid dreaming provides a perspective of possibilities that are not limited to the rules we recognize in waking life. It not only allows the person to experience wild things that feel extremely realistic, but it also directly improves the way their brain functions. Particularly, people who lucid dream have a better connection between their brain's frontopolar cortex and its temporoparietal area. This improvement stems from the way the person's brain has been forced to work during lucid dreaming, which is then carried on into waking life. With this improved connectivity, the person is more inclined towards developing better problem solving skills. One study found that people who have lucid dreams are able to solve up to 25% more problems than those who do not.

The previously discussed hypnagogic and hypnopompic states of sleep—which are often precursors to lucid dreams—can also be used to access heightened creativity. At the beginning of your night, in the moments of transition between wakefulness and sleep, you enter the hypnagogic state. As you drift off, you may see flashes and images in your mind. Oftentimes, these visuals are formed through a combination of various thoughts and memories that you had throughout your day. These thoughts merge with other mental preoccupations (e.g., fantasies and daydreaming), and can sometimes produce slightly odd conceptual ideations. For example, you may find yourself suddenly getting a quirky idea for that business you were thinking about without it actually being realistic. This is the very moment that your brain begins to examine previously programmed information in a different way; because of this, the hypnagogic state often offers visions or thoughts similar to those you had throughout the day but with a weird twist.

This is what gives the hypnagogic state its recognition as being so imaginative; it is a fantastic realm to linger in if you need a burst of creativity. Ideas flow freely as your brain activity eventually eases out of its logic and moves into its dreamy and emotional functioning. If you are trying to solve a particularly complex problem, try and wait for this hypnagogic state to think about it. You may find that solutions come more easily, and you may even come up with options that you previously did not consider.

Just like Mendeleev and his periodic table appearing to him in a dream, Thomas Edison credited his final design for the light bulb on insights he had while being in a hypnagogic state of mind. He used to purposefully induce these sleepy yet creative moments to enhance his innovation. In the afternoons, he would take naps in his armchair in which he would place two metal plates under the armrests and hold ball bearings in his hands. As he drifted off to sleep, he would think about his ideas and research, posing questions to himself in his mind. In the fluid hypnagogic state, his insights would flow much more freely. As he eventually entered a fully asleep state, his body would evidently become immobile, causing him to drop the ball bearings. As they hit the metal plates under the armrests, they would startle him awake and he quickly jotted down any ideas that had come to him. One of these ideas turned out to be the key to his infamous lightbulb design.

As the mind transitions from sleep to wakefulness in the morning, you enter the hypnopompic state. It's easy to miss this phase entirely as we often switch off our alarms and rush to get out of bed. However, if you allow yourself to linger in this fluid, dreamy state for a few extra minutes, you may be surprised at the flashes of insight and inspiration that may occur as your mind transitions to waking life. The hypnopompic state takes place after sleeping the entire night, meaning your brain will have done quite a bit of psychological processing throughout all of the night's dreams, providing you with a clean slate for deep reflection. This is what makes it a period of tremendous insight and clarity.

To gain the most from the hypnopompic state, try not to open your eyes or move your body around. In addition, avoid asking yourself questions that require too much complex thought, as this will wake your mind up far too quickly. Simply notice what is happening in your mind, be aware of whatever thoughts spontaneously pop up, and take note of any new ideas that may occur.

Improved Motor Skills

Sportsmen and women have known for a long time that mentally performing physical skills and routines has the potential to increase their physical ability to do them. In fact, athletes who mentally go through their performance in their minds before an event often do better. In a similar way, lucid dreaming could potentially have a positive impact on physical rehabilitation. Whether you are imagining, dreaming, or physically performing the movement, some of the same parts of your brain are active.

Many believe that lucid dreaming may even be able to accelerate physical healing. This field has been comprehensively examined by leading researchers of lucidity, Ed Kellogg and Robert Waggoner. What they found is that the placebo effect and the ability of the mind to imagine something as real—even if it ultimately is not—is closely linked to being able to physically heal yourself through lucid dreaming. The close interaction between your mind and body, known as the psychosomatic connection, is incredibly powerful. With lucid dreaming, this psychosomatic connection is strengthened, making it easier for the two to work together in favor of physical health.

Physiological changes can be easily induced by your mind. For example, consider how your heart rate rises when you get frightened by something that does not actually pose any threat. Even though the danger is not real, what your mind perceives is happening can still manifest itself as a physical symptom in your body.

Stopping & Preventing Nightmares

Although chronic nightmares are rare, up to 85% of people will experience them every now and then. Usually, they tend to be quite frightening at the time and may even cause us to wake up feeling upset or not rested. Depending on their severity, their aftereffects may even negatively affect a person's mental state for a day or two. In addition, recurring nightmares can turn into a real psychological problem by causing people to be afraid of falling asleep. Not only do nightmares prevent a person from getting an adequate amount of rest, but ultimately, they can also create a sense of helplessness and may cause high levels of stress and anxiety even outside of sleep.

Lucid dreaming can help overcome recurring nightmares as it puts you in control of the dream. Once you recognize that the dream is not real, it loses its fearful component. In fact, as you are now able to control the dream, it can give you a sense of agency and can be used to regain confidence while you are awake as well.

To help people achieve this, psychologists use a technique called imagery rehearsal therapy (IRT) where the patient reimagines a recurring nightmare but chooses a more positive and empowering storyline. This role-play is imagined repeatedly during each therapy session, training the patient's mind to learn to recognize that their nightmare is only a dream and allowing them to use this technique when they are actually asleep to effectively control the dream's outcome.

Chapter 5: Dream World Adventures & Interactions

With such a wide variety of techniques at your very fingertips, the world of lucid dreaming begins to entirely open up to you. By employing these techniques correctly and maintaining patience, you will unlock your own world of lucid dreams. With the right mindset, the impossible quite literally becomes possible and your wildest fantasies are able to be achieved.

Dreams are vivid and rich in emotion. Lucid dreams are absolutely no exception to this. We can do things in our lucid dreams that we would never consider doing while we are awake. Some theorists say that our dreams represent deep unconscious thoughts and motivations that can reflect our darkest wishes. We all have suppressed longings and primitive desires, such as sexual instincts and aggressive tendencies. These show up in our dreamworlds—an effect known as the dream rebound effect. Although our repressions can also manifest themselves in various nasty ways in our real lives, they are often expressed by our minds more freely when we sleep. This can be a particularly healthy way of dealing with urges and desires, especially if you learn to manage them properly within a lucid dream. To maximize the benefits of the dream rebound effect, allow yourself to explore your subconscious in a space that is safe and judgement free.

Such a space can be your lucid dreams. Within them, you are able to control nearly everything. However, this process starts slowly, as many beginners to lucid dreaming may first only become aware of the dream but may struggle to control it. As time goes on, more and more elements of your lucid dream will start to be within your control.

Controlling Your Lucid Dream

Arguably, the hardest part of lucid dreaming is learning how to become aware that you are in a dream. Once you are capable of doing so, you can expect results to flow relatively easily and can begin to work on controlling aspects of your dream. When you are aware that you are dreaming but are unable to control the aspects of what you experience, it is called an uncontrolled lucid dream. In this type of lucid dream, you generally can only control your own actions but nothing outside of them—similar to waking life. This does not indicate any problem in your approach and is a common experience for many beginners. Dream control is generally achieved with practice and more mindfulness.

Although there are many techniques towards improving the control you have over your lucid dreams, they all come down to one key aspect: finding the balance between having conscious control over aspects produced by your subconsciousness. This includes paying close attention to details and evaluating whether or not they are suitable to the desired outcome. By doing so, you are signaling to your brain that all of these details are not being wasted on you and that your conscious self may be ready to take over them. You can also simply speak out loud exactly what it is you want to change in the dream. After a couple times of trying and truly believing that it will happen, the change may just occur. Eventually, these techniques will no longer be necessary, as your unconscious mind lets go of the reins more and more. The following sections describe aspects of your dream that may be within your control, and how you can control them.

People

People are common in many of our dreams, lucid or otherwise. They range from being people that are close to us in real life to third-party characters that do not mean much to us. Whichever they are, sometimes they can help or stall the storyline you desire for your lucid dream. For this reason, sometimes it is helpful to your experience to learn how to control the characters in your story and their actions.

When you want to change something about the people in your lucid dream, begin by asking yourself some insightful questions. Who are the people present? Where or how are they standing? What is each article of clothing they have on? What is their exact facial expression? With such questions, you are increasing your awareness and subtly nudging your subconscious to let you consciously control such aspects.

Lucid dreaming knows no limits. This is directly applicable to people other than yourself as well. For those who are experienced lucid dreamers, they can interchange the characters within their dreams, make them act or respond differently than how they regularly would, or even help them achieve whatever desires they have for the lucid dream itself. Yes, even their appearances and personalities are up for adjustment. The importance here is to not abuse this power and remain diligent in the changes you make.

Known for its therapeutic benefits, lucid dreaming has become a popular way for people to analyze, work on, and experience their relationships from a new perspective. For this reason, many people wish to bring specific people from the outside world into their dreams. Those who wish to do this should have that specific person on their mind before going to bed as well as when they become aware in their dreams. Depending on how familiar their brain is with them, the person can often appear very realistic. To truly serve its purpose of re-examining real-life connections, try to honor their true personality and characteristics.

Environment & Surroundings

One of the most popular aspects of a lucid dream to control is the surroundings. People often wish to experience being somewhere else in the world or even somewhere that does not exist on planet Earth. With lucid dreaming, this is relatively easy to achieve. One step towards garnering more and more control over your lucid dreams is noticing and paying close attention to the surroundings you do not even have control over. In other words, when you find yourself aware in a dream, take in all the details around you. What specific color is the sky? Why do you like it or dislike it?

If you find yourself in surroundings that you wish to change, take notice of all the details that you can manage. Now that your consciousness is focused on such aspects of the surroundings, they can be changed more easily. Make note of how you want your new surroundings to look and invest your energy into this visualization. The changes may occur slowly, with each aspect being broken down and built back up in the way you have envisioned it. At other times, all of the changes you want to see will appear all at once.

A common method used to change surroundings in lucid dreams is to simply imagine yourself going to a place. For example, if you find yourself in your own home but would like to be in a castle, you can imagine such a castle being just around the block. In this fashion, you exit your house in your dream and make your way to the location where you have created the castle. If this is a little too mundane, or if you want to be in a completely different environment altogether, you could even teleport or fly to your new destination. Flying is a very popular method of travel in lucid dreams, both due to its expeditious estimated time of arrival and its impossibility in the real world.

Although this is commonly more accessible to avid lucid dreamers, the use of portals is also up for grabs. Similar to teleportation, the person simply imagines a portal in front of them that will take them to whatever environment they wish for.

Storyline

In order to test themselves or simply broaden their experiences, people who lucid dream love to control the storyline. The storyline of a lucid dream incorporates aspects of both people and the environment. By learning to control those two aspects, the control of the storyline also becomes available to you. The only thing left to learn is how to control the unfolding of events that have nothing to do with you.

For example, if for whatever reason you wish to experience a more movie-like plotline, you would have to learn how to make events happen that do not rely on your actions. To achieve controlling the storyline on this scale, start with something smaller at first. For example, attempt flying through the sky and simultaneously having birds fly next to you. With enough time and power, those skills will translate to events that can be as dramatic as you wish.

What Not to Do

The best way to count on having a positive experience from lucid dreams is making sure you are aware of the right and wrong things to do. As lovely and beneficial as lucid dreaming can be, it still has the potential to be unpleasant or end too quickly when choosing to perform certain incorrect actions.

The first suggestion is to avoid doing dangerous or highly unlikely tasks too quickly in your lucid dreaming journey. For example, if you attempt to fly in your very first lucid dream, you may end up falling, which can be both disappointing and frightening. The same goes for any actions that would be completely impossible in the real world. Save the extremes for a time when you are more advanced with your skills. Another thing to avoid doing is closing your eyes unless you want yourself to wake up. Oftentimes, closing your eyes in a lucid dream is used as a technique to end the dream and wake up in real life. If you close your eyes for too long, you risk that happening. This, however, can be beneficial to remember if you do want to end a lucid dream for any reason.

As mentioned before, many people choose to include certain characters in their lucid dreams but not others. The only danger of picking and choosing people you already know in your life is that your connection within the lucid dream does not represent reality. In other words, if you focus all your lucid dreaming on one connection, you may end up with a relationship that does not translate into the real world. If you do choose to include people you know in your lucid dreams, make sure to not overindulge.

The last thing to avoid is arguably the most important: negative thoughts. This may be quite obvious at this point, but thinking negative thoughts may prompt some unpleasant experiences to manifest themselves. After all, lucid dreaming is basically experiencing the depths of your own mind but consciously. Therefore, the undesirable thoughts that you may end up focusing on may cause things to go sour. If you wish to experience something that you are scared of, things may actually get out of hand. This is once again tied to the importance of being in a great headspace prior to setting off into your dream world and focusing on gaining enriching experiences, not traumatizing ones.

Chapter 6: Advanced Lucid Dreaming Techniques

As with any skill, there are basic techniques to first get started and there are those that tend to be only applicable to people who are already experienced. This makes lucid dreaming become a never-ending journey on which you will discover more and more opportunities. In fact, many people who have been practicing lucid dreaming for years or even a decade believe they have only scratched the surface of everything it has to offer. After all, the mind is limitless and even a century's worth of lucid dreaming experiences will not be representative of all that is possible. It may seem like a drag, having to wait so much time to truly get the most out of lucid dreaming, but to anyone who sees its true value, it is worth the wait.

The good news is, the more you get to know your own subconscious mind, the more you will be able to do. Once you are past the preliminary steps of learning to become aware in a dream and moving on to garnering control, dive into the techniques that will offer you a whole new set of skills to use.

Improving Proficiency

Lucid dreaming can seem like quite a futile thing, especially at first; your actions and certain events may not unfold in the way that you want them to. Even worse, you might be having the experience of a lifetime and then accidentally wake yourself up from it because you have gotten too excited. In a lucid dream, our brains function in a state of half-consciousness; they help us create a world within our own heads and give us just enough conscious control to be able to enjoy this world attentively. However, with too much emotional stimulation, parts of our brain may become so alert that they break us away from our dream worlds and back into reality. Extreme emotions simply overpower the unconsciousness that is responsible for our lucid dreams.

Another reason for a dream to possibly end prematurely is the person becoming far too focused on the world outside of their lucid dream. For example, they may think it is so fascinating that they have become lucid that they keep thinking about the fact that their physical body is lying in bed. Basically, giving your awareness to anything other than the dream at hand for too long may cause it to fall apart. There is quite a thin line between forgetting to be involved in your dream long enough to maintain lucidity and becoming so involved with the dream that you risk losing it. The trick here is dream stabilization.

When you feel as though your lucidity is slipping away and you are at risk of having your dream collapse, employ the dream stabilization technique. With dream stabilization, you learn how to ground yourself in the dream to prevent yourself from exerting an overwhelming amount of emotion and letting your awareness fade. This includes grounding yourself in the dream with the following techniques:

- Examine your hands. If you feel like the dream bubble you find yourself aware of is becoming less and less profound, look at the palms of your hands. While the rest of the scenery slowly becomes more and more clear, focus only on your own hands. Eventually, the dream may regain its clarity and return back to its normal state.

- Rub your hands together. If the setting around you seems clear enough but you feel as though your awareness is still not quite as strong, rub one of your hands against the other. Although the science behind this is not quite explained, many believe that this provides a life-like sensation that can be used to remind your mind of your lucidity.

- Spin around to reset the scene. When things are getting a little too fuzzy, you can attempt to return things back to normal by spinning in your dream. By spinning, the environment around you goes blurry, allowing it to recreate itself once you stop. However, make sure you spin only enough to reset the scene; spinning for too long may cause you to become even more out of touch with your dream world.

- Focus on being attentive. Just like when you first learned the techniques to control the things around you, giving all your attention to the small details that surround you can also help you maintain just the right amount of lucidity. Notice the sights, smells, and any other sensations you may be experiencing.

- Speak it into existence. Talking to yourself is not just an action you can do when you are alone in the waking world. By stating out loud "more lucidity" or something of the sort, you are actively reminding your mind that you do not want to lose awareness.

- Avoid lying down for too long. Similar to the idea that keeping your eyes closed for too long may cause you to wake up, so can lying down. By spending too much of your time relaxing horizontally in your lucid dream, your mind may match it with your physical body and wake you up as well. Movement is one of the keys towards maintaining a solid amount of lucidity.

Beyond the Basics

So far, we have discussed how to solidify your presence within the lucid dream and how to employ some very basic methods of beginning to increase your level of control. It is important not to skip any of those steps, as they are a crucial foundation for more advanced techniques associated with controlling lucid dreams. The initial techniques for becoming lucid in a dream and beginning to control certain aspects of it are meant to be mastered before moving on to more powerful and complex strategies. However, once you become skilled with the basics of lucid dreaming, you are encouraged to start implementing advanced methods of control that will let you make your lucid dream even more interesting.

There are five advanced categories that are most popular for avid lucid dreamers. They include:

1. **Verbal strategies.** Similar to speaking to your own mind to remain lucid, communicating verbally directly to your surroundings and other characters within the dream may help you strengthen your control over them. In addition to speaking out loud such as 'Come with me' or 'I will make that cloud disappear' you have to believe that you have the power to make what you are saying truly happen.

2. **Using objects or the surroundings.** As previously mentioned, many avid lucid dreamers use portals to travel

to a different environment. A similar concept applies here—you can assign certain 'powers' to an object of your choice to help you control whatever it is you desire. For example, it can be an object as classic as a magic wand, or it can be more unique to you such as a certain stone or garment of clothing. Once you are lucid in your dream, you can either find or make the object of your choice appear. Then, make it consciously clear that this specific object will be able to fulfill your wishes. For example, if you designate a wand as your object, you will then expect your desires to come true when you use the wand in a specific way. With this technique, you cement your conviction of being capable of control by believing that this object is specifically used to exert your desires.

3. **Bodily strategies.** This is quite a direct technique that can help trick your mind into letting your consciousness control the dream. For example, some people who wish to fly may start jumping into the air over and over again until they reach the point of flying. Others may use their body to even control aspects outside of themselves; they might use their hands to signal objects to move—similar to the concept of telekinesis. Sometimes, you can even try changing the entire environment by moving your body to facilitate certain changes. Try moving your arms above your head to change the direction of the clouds or swiping them around yourself to change the color scheme of the sky entirely.

4. **Emotional management.** People have found that having control over your own emotions in a lucid dream may be one of the most powerful techniques in inducing certain changes. If a third-party character is acting outside of your control, react in a positive way rather than

responding negatively. For example, hug them and exert a positive emotion of acceptance and satisfaction. To your surprise, their actions may now be far more controllable than before. Some speculate that emotion management strategies are effective because everything we see in a lucid dream is a manifestation of certain aspects of ourselves. With acceptance, you prove that you do not hate these aspects of yourself, but instead are open to changing them.

5. **Other methods.** Beyond the four methods described above is a category that includes every other strategy unique to different dreamers. This category includes other methods such as visualization of the changes you desire or even embodying the aspects you would like to see. For example, embodying a third-party character you would like to interact with may summon them to appear.

Let Go and Dream

We are all capable of positive change and most of us even desire it. The demands of our daily lives often get in the way of such change being easily accessible to us. While some people turn to potentially dangerous substances or safer options such as seeking support from loved ones, lucid dreaming provides us with another option: to facilitate these changes through our own mind and our mind alone. This is perhaps the most enticing aspect of lucid dream exploration—the endless possibilities coupled with the fact that the environment you find yourself in is one completely free of judgment. In fact, even the mundaneness you once found in your regular life may be erased once you have been introduced to everything that your mind is capable of. All that is left to do is start; ease yourself into the world your own subconscious has created for you and learn how managing it will provide benefits long after you wake up.

Oftentimes, people who first start to lucid dream get caught up in exploring relatively subtle experiences that they simply cannot explore in real life, such as visiting a vacation spot or hiking up a gorgeous mountain trail. However, the more familiar they get with their lucid dreaming capabilities, the more opportunities present themselves. They begin living out all of their fantasies, no matter how otherworldly they may be. It is a win-win situation in which you increasingly connect with yourself while expanding your experiences far more than most can even imagine.

Whether you align more with Freud's, Jung's, LaBerge's or any other professional's point of view, the importance of our underlying psychology is indisputable. We have much left to learn in relation to even ourselves; the darkest parts of our mind generally stay dormant while we are awake but may very well show themselves in our dreams. Psychologists, neuroscientists, and oneirologists have provided humanity with countless theories and hypotheses that may help encourage us to get to know ourselves. We leave our lucid dreams with a stronger understanding of our own repressed emotions and desires. Why leave it up to chance when you have the power within yourself to steer yourself into the experiences you desire?

Allow yourself to finally express everything you harbor freely. Once you conquer the initial fear of your own mind, you learn to accept it. When you get to know every aspect of yourself—no matter how surprising it may be—you learn to embrace it. Truly, there are enough mysteries in lucid dreaming to fill a library. However, most of them you can, and should, discover yourself. Through the techniques you just learned, all this—and more—is possible. Allow yourself to dream and miracles will surely follow.

www.ingramcontent.com/pod-product-compliance
Lightning Source LLC
LaVergne TN
LVHW021736060526
838200LV00052B/3316